I'm Sorry...

I didn't know.

By

Suzanne Woolley

I'm Sorry..I Didn't Know
by Suzanne Woolley

ISBN 978-0-9957078-3-2

First published in 2018 by SanRoo Publishing 2018 in Leicestershire, UK.

All Rights Reserved.

Copyright© Suzanne Woolley 2018

The right of Suzanne Woolley to be identified as the author of this work has been asserted by her in accordance with the Copyright, Designs and Patents Act 1988. No portion of this publication should be reproduced without prior permission.

Cover designed by Sandra Pollock
Cover Photography by Luke Smith

Proudly published July 2018 in Leicester, UK,
by SanRoo Publishing,
26 Bramble Way, Leicester, LE3 2GY, U.K.
www.sanroopublishing.co.uk

CONTENTS

Acknowledgements *4*

You're definitely not the little girl you used to be! *5*

How are you coping today? .... *6 - 7*

What's for dinner? .... *8 - 10*

Why didn't you leave? *11*

Why don't you let it go? .... *12 - 13*

Where have you been? .... *14 - 15*

You are so strong .... *16 - 17*

I'm sorry for your loss .... *18 - 19*

Why do you even still care about him? *20*

I Was Wrong *21*

Oh, Wow, BBW *22*

Why the fuck would you screenshot that? *23*

What were you wearing? .... *24 - 26*

Why didn't you warn me? .... *27 - 28*

I'm sorry I didn't know .... *29 - 30*

About *31*

Acknowledgements

I would like to thank my mum – Janet Woolley, for loving and raising me despite my many rebellious periods and twisted moments, and still supporting and loving me to this very day. My siblings, Christine and Alan.

I would like to thank my niece Olivia and my 'niece' Mimi for showing me endless unconditional love and brightening up my life.

My friends who have suffered through these moments with me, pulled me through and relived them with me: Chelsea, Poppyann, Schlam, Kelly, Slice, Graeme, Ryan (honestly this list could go on).

I would like to thank the people who never say no to reading my poems and providing insight to make them better: Claire, Andrew, Charlotte, Sandra, Jonathan.

I would especially like to thank the wonderful team at SanRoo Publishing for giving me the opportunity, allowing me to express myself and reach others.

As well as the Leicester literary scene, especially Some – Antics for warmly welcoming me every month to share in the awesome poetry.

I would like to thank my laptop for standing strong in its over use.

I would like to thank the variety of people who have encouraged me throughout my life.

Lastly, I would like to thank the myriad of people I have met, who have made my life difficult enough that I needed to write poetry about it. (I forgive you all)

"You're definitely not the little girl you used to be!"

praise be to the girl
I used to be
for she brought me here
strapped to her back
in tattered rags
stumbling through the garden
catching on the thorns
blood running down her thighs
feeding the pricks with her pain

arms wrapped around her neck
I suck the vitality from her
to grow incredibly large
until her body bows
and her back snaps,

flesh hanging in ribbons from her bones
crawling forward
over shadowed
she curls

I pick her up
to carry her on my back,
as she carries the others
until I am born again.

"Yeah, I guess I've changed quite a bit."

"How are you coping today?"

a smile chart
for an absent child
black eyes
resting, elevated
on rounded cheeks,
a curling thin line
joins one side to the other.

the yellow circle
lines up against red and blue –
ticking away, the days
my own lips curl to my cheeks

I wish I was taught
it is ok to be sad
years of therapy tell me
that the age 7,
is my impact year
of fuckery

that year spent getting swallowed
into the belly of crowds,
and weekend breaks
to the prison

I wish I was taught
It is ok to be sad

a smile chart
for an empty child
my head against brick
vandalised with a bloody nose,
to settle the riot inside

locked in a room
with rainbow padding
so my damage
would never be external.

I wish I was taught
It is ok to be sad

days forcing my lips to curl
with black eyes
elevated on cheeks

sticker rewards
lined up
with smiling faces

I wish I was taught
it is ok to be sad
then,
I wouldn't be a great liar.

(Smiling)
"I'm ok"

"What's for dinner?"

chubby fingers
wrapped around the wooden spoon
wrapped with spaghetti

arm twirling
sauce splattering
pushing on her tippy toes.

the door slams
tired and weary
he slumps a bag on the counter

"Daddy!"

whistling through gappy teeth
fingers reaching
pulling on trouser legs.

he unbuttons the collar
claws at the tie
inhales from drowning.

"Where is she? Upstairs?"

climbing the stairs
palms down
he reaches the peak.

I close the door.

the music cranked
she rests on my forearm
with her hand in my palm.

we call on the sun
and sway along
to the Beatles.

pounding footsteps
flying down the stairs
the front door slams.

the second footsteps creep
pushing on tippy toes
door handle rattles
unveiling a face
tired and weary

"Mummy!"

whistling through gappy teeth
fingers reaching
pulling on trouser legs.

lifted to her chest
nose nestled into neck
then their eyes meet.

"Where's daddy?"

she doesn't ask again.

sun breaches through the clouds
gathering on tiled floors
and we sway along
to the Beatles

arm twirling
sauce splattering
pushing on her tippy toes.

"So, what are we having?"

cheeks rising
whistling through gappy teeth
fingers reaching

"S'ghetti!"

"Why didn't you leave?"

Purple butterflies
cluster just beneath my ribs,
painted by your hands
blackening with every day.

with a kiss
They burrow under my skin
swarm around my stomach
racing to break through my teeth

my body shrinking
They grow with your words.
when the sounds were ice
They would pull out their stingers
wasps in disguise
my chest, their target

your hands encircle my wrists
making rainbow bracelets
reminding me that I was lucky.

I was lucky.

sorry after sorry, after sorry,
whispered to the butterflies
that brown with age
fade into my skin
sealed with tears
from cocoons in your head

this time it would be different
this time You would be different.

"It wasn't always like that"

"Why don't you let it go?"

I had spent too long
keeping secrets
so I didn't ruin you.

I had listened to your stories
watched your mind play tricks
watched you laugh at yourself
taking punches for the punchlines.

I had talked to you at 3am
so you knew someone
gave you some worth

I was ready to forgive you
when you said you chose me
"because there was more of me"
"and you can"

I was ready to forgive you,
when you came back into the room
drunk
and climbed into my bed.

I was ready to forgive you
when you didn't leave.

I was ready to forgive you
when you draped your arm over me
to grab my boob
while I was sleeping
or at least pretending to.

I was ready to forgive you
when the sun sliced through the curtains

and you were still there.

I was ready to forgive you
when you stayed in that room
spoke to no one
when a darkness invaded you.

I was ready to forgive you
when you just left.

I was ready to forgive you
when you didn't talk to me again.

I was ready to forgive you
when I heard you stopped drinking.

I was ready to forgive you
for keeping it a secret
so people do not think less of you
for me keeping it a secret
so they do not think less of me.

"I am ready to let it go, if you can forgive yourself"

"Where have you been?"

I am the master of self destruction
10 ticks always from an explosion,
leaving a trail of devastation.

see it isn't just about physically scarring yourself.
self destruction has many faces,
my shadow perfecting the art of sabotage.

it's listening as someone you love,
tells you they love you,
and getting drunk and kissing another
because the only thing harder than rejection,
is the knowledge that you're poison.

it's walking in the dark down a dangerous unlit path,
in the hope that it might make you feel fear or something
and you still feel nothing

it's watching endless shows
about weight loss and healthy lifestyles,
promising yourself
"Tomorrow will be the day"
but you know, it's just an excuse to eat your cupboards empty.

it's having money,
knowing you have bills to pay
but telling yourself "Girl… treat yo'self"

it's accumulating a mass of friends
not talking to them,
and getting angry because they won't talk to you.

it's shutting yourself off,

getting confused, convincing yourself
what you feel is empathy
because these can't actually be YOUR feelings.

it's not just text,
it's 45 texts and 3 phone calls, a Voice recording, 5
Facebook messages and a multiple rewatch of their
snapchat story,
because they're ignoring you, because of that thing you did,
5 years ago,
to someone else.

it's hating yourself everyday
neglecting your body,
avoiding mirrors,
eating to be sick
throwing meds down the toilet
not going to meetings
cutting up your clothes
breaking doors and walls
standing on the roof of buildings

it's pushing everyone out of the blast radius,
shaking alone in the centre,
telling yourself you're better off alone.

"Sorry, I was busy"

"You are so strong"

If Strength is
eating around others
starving alone
convincing my mum
I'd had a big lunch
apple slices
and carrot sticks

I'd rather be weak.

if Strength is
walking
marching down
dark alleys
counting the calories
burning them off
returning from the walk
at midnight

I'd rather be weak

if Strength is
nobody noticing
how fast
you're wasting away
because there is more
to waste

I'd rather be weak

if Strength is
smiling everyday
laughing at
the claws in my chest

the memories
rattling the door handles

I'd rather be weak

if Strength is
taking myself
placing her under a lamp
examining every scratch
every chip
every crack
and painting over them

I'd rather be weak.

if Strength is
standing by my man
plastering my cuts
hiding my bruises
to help his 'recovery'

I'd rather be weak

if Strength is
tearing down friends
to get ahead
rising higher
on a mountain
of scape goats

I'd rather be weak

the strength you see,
is laced with poisons
I drank from its chalice
melting my vocal chords

left only with
silence .

"I'm really trying this time"

"I'm sorry for your loss"

every seat filled
with strangers.
relatives, I have never met.

come to mourn
a crownless king,
a 'good man'

passing my hand
around like a parcel,
to shake the hands
of aliens.

they sit in black
to pray –
to pay respects
to a man
they no longer knew

I shoo them away
with a wave
their bellies filled
content with their respects
to tie away any guilt

they do not linger
Do not invest time
into the woman I am now
Did not invest time
into the girl I was
Did not invest time
into a dying man
but give a pocket of time
to a dead man.

Ants lining
out the door
the chorus repeating
as though I were illiterate.

"you spoke so well"

"Thank you"

"Why do you even still care about him?"

I'm tired of believing
that I don't deserve happiness
that I don't deserve you.

I raised you to the sky
like an offering to the gods
returning you to where you belonged,
my feet sinking in quicksand
returning to where I belong

I was wrong.

I should not have raised your bar so high,
that even being your friend
gave me a fear of heights
and falling for you felt endless

as I rose you up
I buried myself
swallowed by dirt.

For you,
we walked together
our feet touched the level ground
tapping out a rhythm of our own
bandaging each other's blisters
using each other as a crutch
carrying each other until the path ends
completely the same.

I was wrong
Then you pushed me out
I fell to collide with the dirt I knew.
its darkness welcomed me
like a worn mattress
dipping in the middle with my weight.
it had not changed its shape
and I slotted in place,
pushing deeper.

you had disappeared
and I had never felt so worthless.

I'm tired of believing
that I didn't deserve happiness,
that I didn't deserve you.

I was wrong.

"Because I do"

"Oh, Wow, BBW"

Big
Beautiful
Woman.

Why can't I just be a
Beautiful
Woman?

or do you intend on using

SBW (Skinny Beautiful Woman)
ABW (Average Beautiful Woman)
TBW (Tall Beautiful Woman)
LBW (Little Beautiful Woman)
BBM (Big Beautiful Man)
SBM (Skinny Beautiful Man)
ABM (Average Beautiful Man)
TBM (Tall Beautiful Man)
LBM (Little Beautiful Man)
BBP (Big Beautiful Person)
SBP (Skinny Beautiful Person)
ABP (Average Beautiful Person)
TBP (Tall Beautiful Person)
LBP (Little Beautiful Person)
DBP (Disabled Beautiful Person)
BPEM (Beautiful Person of Ethnic Minority)

and this list could go on...

but if you just wanna say
"Oh, Wow, You're surprisingly pretty for a fat bird"

"Just fuck off"

"Why the fuck would you screenshot that?"

Here is a tip –
if you are going to send
a picture of your dick
to anyone (but especially me),
unsolicited,
be prepared,
That picture of your penis
is popping up on the phones
of my pals like a weasel
so we can laugh
at your neatly trimmed pubes
and the fact that you just decided
that all females want to see it,
the manhood you are so proud of
that you pop it out
like a handmade jack in the box
for us to gawk at
until our knickers simulate
the pot you put under a leaking roof,
filling up way faster than anticipated.
Let me tell you my knickers
are drier than my eczema
riddled hands
in winter,
without gloves,
when I have run out of moisturiser.

Then you panic
as you are informed
the image has been
saved

"Maybe you should send me a picture of your face before your dick"

"What were you wearing?"

85% of those sexually assaulted
do not report the crime
I am 1 out of 172,266
for that year
for this country

this is not including –
those who never knew,
those who believe it was ok,
those who just do not understand,
those who never seek any help.

Who can blame them?
When only 5.7% of those reported
are convicted.

2/3rds,
2/3rds of the population
can blame them.
want to blame them.

flicking our hair, smiling, flirting
means we are not victims.
revealing more than 30% of our bodies
means we are not victims.
being in a relationship
means we are not victims.
lying passed out on a bed
means we are not victims –

when a 16 stone body
pushes down into me
and I'm swallowed by a mattress
suffocating with words
persuading me
that I should be happy.

Because I never said
the word "No"
means I am not a victim.

and a panel of men,
cannot understand
do not understand
will not understand
that I never said yes either.

I was never taught to shout
"No!"
as if it ripped through my vagina
and broke through my lips

the blood under my nails
are not enough.
the bruises on my wrists and thighs
are not enough.
Because he said that I like it rough.

they were never forced
to leave their bodies
as it were invaded
colonised by his sperm
as they broke through my skin
wriggling through my veins
clotting to stop my thoughts
as I rock… curled…
in the corner of my brain
not feeling anymore.

when he's finished

rolls on his side
to check his phone
my body moves to the shower
where it stays
hoping the water is acid
willing it to burn off all the layers
his body had touched.

Who can blame them?
When only 5.7% of those reported
are convicted.

"Why does it matter?"

"Why didn't you warn me?"

when his foot left my door,
when it never came back,
I undid the belt
that had been wrapped around
my neck
and secured it around my waist

I exhaled the hurricane
That brewed in my chest
where he left it.

I should have flooded
this house with a tsunami of tears
but I barely made a puddle.
prayed for amnesia.

passing my reflection
I could still see him
in the bruises not yet healed
in my eyes not yet blinded
in my veins not yet clean

I should have talked
to the world, my family, the police
but I could barely think
locking the memories away.

I should have

When he locked onto you
Set his missiles to launch

I should have

When he pulled you like a marionette
And you learned to hate your friends

I should have

When nobody heard from you
And you were just a name in a story
Of some girl we used to know.

I should have

But I was afraid.

I didn't want to be on his radar,
I'm hidden in a background of people
who had no idea.
I didn't want to be a crazy ex
with her crazy stories
I didn't want to be a victim
for stories I had nearly forgotten.

when they saved you
and you were braver than I
telling the world of him

"I should have, and I'm sorry"

"I'm sorry I didn't know"

We all have stories
we don't want to tell,

have songs
that could give you nightmares,

are rattled
by words,
by sounds,
by gestures,
by touches

are afraid to think
afraid to feel.

We all have skulls
piled in our wardrobes
fearing opening the door
to grab a scarf
and them rolling onto the feet of our loved ones.

We all have scars
that we made ourselves
by not letting our wounds heal properly,

We all think they're ugly.

we all open our mouths sometimes
willing the words to come out
but just croaking.

We all have a backlog
of wrong turns
and many trampled paths.

I have some stories
that are hard to tell
and they thickened my edges
and make me flinch

They bring more tears to others
who cannot imagine
who feel deeper for me than I ever felt for myself
who are sorry for the actions of others

"It is ok, I forgive you"

About the Author

Suzanne Woolley is a Leicester based poet with a number of published works.
She has a BA in Creative Writing and is currently working towards her MA.
Many years teaching, writing, and performing within the literary world has given her a strong voice within the community.
This collection of poems was created from her experiences throughout her life, exploring a variety of different issues.

SanRoo Publishing

To find out more about SanRoo Publishing visit our website at:

www.sanroopublishing.co.uk

Follow us on Facebook @acalltowrite

or on Twitter @SanRooWriters

SanRoo Publishing
Is part of
Inspiring You C.I.C.

26 Bramble Way, Leicester, LE3 2GY
Registered Company No. : 10213814

www.ingramcontent.com/pod-product-compliance
Lightning Source LLC
Chambersburg PA
CBHW070443010526
44118CB00014B/2171